Vanessa and Virginia

A Play in One Act

by E. H. Wright

Published by Playdead Press 2013

© E.H. Wright

E.H. Wright has asserted her rights under the Copyright, Design and Patents Act, 1988, to be identified as the author of this work.

A CIP catalogue record for this book is available from the British Library.

ISBN 978-0-9575266-2-4

Playdead Press
www.playdeadpress.com

Biography

Dr E. H. Wright is a senior lecturer at Bath Spa University. Her research is primarily concerned with the modernist writer Virginia Woolf and early twentieth-century theatre. Her work on Woolf includes biography, articles and a monograph on Woolf's connections with contemporary drama. *Vanessa and Virginia*, based on the novel by Susan Sellers, is her debut play.

Vanessa and Virginia was first presented at the Société d'Études Woolfiennes International Conference in Aix-en-Provence on 17th and 18th September 2010 by Moving Stories supported by the AHRC. The first performances included the following cast:

Vanessa Bell   Kitty Randle
Virginia Woolf   Sarah Fullagar

Directed by Emma Gersch
Produced by Claudine Eastwood
Setting designed by Kate Unwin and students of the Bath Spa University Paintworks

The play was performed in London at the Riverside Studios from 26th March to 14th April 2013 with the following cast:

Vanessa Bell   Kitty Randle
Virginia Woolf   Alice Frankham

Directed by Emma Gersch
Designed by Kate Unwin
Produced by Samuel Julyan
Music by Jeremy Thurlow

Characters

Vanessa Bell
Virginia Woolf

A note on the text

Vanessa and Virginia based on the acclaimed novel by Susan Sellers, was first performed at the Société d'Études Woolfiennes International Conference in Aix-en-Provence on 17th and 18th September 2010 to a mixture of Bloomsbury scholars and the general public. The play then went on to a European tour culminating in a run at The Riverside Studios in Hammersmith, London. Over the course of the tour the script evolved and the set altered to accommodate the needs of various venues. This script was the basis of the original production performed in Aix, though certain changes were made for that particular performance some of which I have retained here. Small but significant alterations to the script were partly the work of the original cast and crew to whom I am indebted. I feel that this version of the script offers the greatest potential to future directors who will inevitably wish to 'make it their own' in the course of production.

Thanks should be given to Moving Stories Theatre Company and in particular the wonderful director Emma Gersch, the designer Kate Unwin, the production manager George Seal, the composer Jeremy Thurlow and the actresses Kitty Randle, Sarah Fullagar and Alice Frankham who have made their own marks on this text. Thanks are also due to the great and gracious Susan Sellers who gave her blessing and tireless support to this adaptation.

On stage are a screen and two boxes or chairs which can be moved by the actors. The image on the screen (which could be projected or painted by the actors) should reflect the mood of the moment unfolding in front of it. The mood and often the ages of the characters changes at each scene transition marked in the text. Scene transitions are signalled by the changing image and music. The actresses move seamlessly between scenes and ages. All props are set on the stage. Virginia should remain present on stage throughout, though at times she is not engaged in the action. Unlike Vanessa who tells, as well as plays out, the story of their relationship, Virginia never directly addresses the audience.

Vanessa seated writing. She is a woman of about 70.

VANESSA: Childhood. I am lying on my back on the grass. Thoby is lying next to me, his warm flank pressing into my side.

[Looking up] My angel disappears. I recognise your snake-green eyes.

For a moment I think I see your face, young, impish, grinning at me as I write. *[Takes ribbons from pockets and scatters them across the stage]*

My memories are as tangled as the reels of thread and fragments of cloth in Mother's sewing basket which I loved to tip out onto the nursery floor.

Scene transition. Vanessa and Virginia are aged 4 and 6 years old. Virginia enters, creeping up on Vanessa with a large sheet of fabric which she uses to catch Vanessa. They play together. Suddenly they stand to attention as though waiting for their mother's approval.

VANESSA: Always, Thoby goes first. I watch him pulled into the curve of mother's arm, closing my eyes to imagine the silky feel of her dress, her smell of lavender and Pears soap. Yet when Adrian is relinquished with a kiss and Mother holds out her hand to you it is as if a promise has been broken. I am the eldest. I should come before you. *[Bitterly]* You seem to spend an eternity in her arms and when Mother praises you I wonder what would happen if a spark from the fire were to catch your petticoat.

Scene transition.

VANESSA: *[Facing Virginia]* Our faces are imperfect replicas of each other, as if the painter were trying to capture the same person from different angles. Your face is prettier than mine, your features finer, your eyes a whirligig of quick lights. You are my natural ally in my dealings with the world. I adore the way you watch me accomplish the things you cannot yet achieve, but I

8

do not yet see your frustration, your desire
to catch up and topple me.

Scene transition. Vanessa and Virginia aged 8 and 6.

VIRGINIA: Who do you like best, Mother or Father?

VANESSA: *[Pauses with amazement]* Mother.

VIRGINIA: I prefer Father.

VANESSA: Father? How can you possibly like Father best? He's always so difficult to please.

VIRGINIA: At least he's not vague

VANESSA: But Mother is…

VIRGINIA: Is what?

VANESSA: *[Quietly]* Beautiful.

VIRGINIA: *[Contemptuously]* What does that count for? Mother doesn't know as much as Father; she doesn't read as much. At least when Father settles on something you know he isn't going to be called away. *[Pause]* Well, at least we needn't fight about who we like.

9

VANESSA: *[To the audience]* Not for the first time, I find myself fearing where your cleverness will lead.

Scene transition. *Vanessa and Virginia lie as though in bed. They are aged 12 and 10.*

VANESSA: We lie in our beds watching the darkness. I close my eyes to conjure the moonlight and listen for Mother's footsteps on the stairs. There are guests tonight and we have helped her dress. *[Calls out]* Mother? *[To Virginia]* I wonder if the dinner is a success?

VIRGINIA: *[Yawning]* She will tell us all about it tomorrow.

VANESSA: Not for our amusement though. She'll want us to benefit from the example. We are always second. *[Thinking she hears her mother she calls out]* Mother?

VIRGINIA: She's not coming Nessa. *[Clearing her throat to tell a story]* A bedtime adventure. Mrs MacCavity was most surprised one morning to discover that the family had run out of eggs. *[Continues in a whisper which underscores Vanessa]*

10

VANESSA: *[To the audience]* I let your words weave their spell. Soon I have forgotten the darkness and Mother's broken promise. I am caught up in your world of make-believe. I fall asleep dreaming of hobgoblins and golden hens and eggs fried for breakfast with plenty of frizzle. *[Falls asleep]*

Virginia steals the amethyst necklace that is hanging around Vanessa's neck while she is sleeping.

VIRGINIA: *[Holding up the amethyst necklace]* This one is for Mother. Mother who loves the beautiful Nessa more than she has time to say.

Vanessa reaches for the necklace.

VIRGINIA: *[Chanting]* Nessa the bountiful, Nessa the good. If only Mother wasn't so busy. *[She taunts Vanessa with the necklace who tries to snatch it angrily]* *[Referring to herself]* Ah, now what have we here? A poor, orphaned goat, bleating most piteously for her dolphin Mother.

VANESSA: Billy Goat!

VIRGINIA: Someone who would rather Ness didn't scold quite so much, someone who wishes Ness would stop drawing and put her lovely arms around her and pet her. *[Vanessa chases Virginia]* Goats are good at climbing, remember. And at leaping. *[Virginia climbs onto a chair and leaps from it. Vanessa catches her and violently takes the necklace]*

Vanessa and Virginia freeze as though caught being naughty.

VIRGINIA: What you see before you, Mother is a devil *[Bows]* and a saint! *[Gestures to Vanessa]*

VANESSA: Instead of chastising you, Mother laughs. That evening your phrase is repeated to Father, who claps his hands at your wit. Soon he is calling me 'saint' and winking at you. George, Gerald, even Thoby join in the taunt. Any suggestion that you might be a devil seems to slip from everyone's mind.

Scene transition.

VANESSA: We crowd into the carriage that will take us to the station, our arms full of books, spades, butterfly nets, cricket bats, tins of crayons, straw hats. On holiday in St Ives we do not keep our rigid London schedules. Even Father appears released from the relentless burden of work that oppresses him in London. It is here I come alive. Shut up all year like Persephone, it is a sudden baptism of light. Like a starved prisoner I drink it in.

Vanessa dances or paints her sense of freedom wildly. She continues to speak as she moves.

All summer long I try to bottle the light, store it up, capture it in my sketches, so that I can take it back to London with me and feed on it during the dreary winter months. In St Ives I am at liberty to draw and paint all day. It is here that I do my first serious painting, my sister Stella guiding my hand as I discover new shapes to fill the dark.

Scene transition.

VANESSA: Back in London we become each other's mirrors, but there is an arrogance in our complicity. We have no guide to direct us, no check on our imaginings and delusions. Metamorphosed in the mill of your descriptive genius, the weaknesses and

13

foibles of those around us become props to shore up our own faltering self-images.

Virginia jumps onto a box or a chair.

VIRGINIA: *[Laughing and pointing off stage]* She looks like something from the museum that hasn't been successfully preserved! *[Vanessa giggles]*

VANESSA: Look at them dressed like parakeets! *[Virginia laughs]*

VIRGINIA: Shall we dance? *[They bow and curtsey to each other and waltz]*

VANESSA: We are trained to be ladies. Performing monkeys. How was it you put it once?

VIRGINIA: We learn to venerate the angel of virtue, whose selflessness is such that she has no requirements of her own.

VANESSA: She is paraded constantly before us, our goal and unrelenting goad. Little wonder, then, that you eventually murdered her, stabbed the point of your pen in her perfect, impossible breast.

14

Scene transition. Vanessa and Virginia hold hands and cross the stage. Vanessa is 14, Virginia is 13.

VANESSA: At the doorway we hold hands. All of our brothers - George, Gerald, Thoby, Adrian – and our sister, Stella, are there. I bend down to kiss Mother's forehead, and hear the awful drag of her breathing. I need her to speak to me. I need her to explain what is happening. I need her to tell me she loves me. Her eyes remain resolutely closed. Father lets out a great, raging howl and you depart from sanity.

Scene transition. Virginia climbs onto a box or chair with arms out-stretched.

VIRGINIA: *[Screaming]* If you come any closer I'll jump through the windowpane.

VANESSA: Please calm yourself Billy.

VIRGINIA: *[Calming]* It will dissolve us all.

Vanessa reaches up, takes Virginia's hand and leads her down.

VANESSA: Would you like me to close the curtains?

VIRGINIA: Yes. *[Pause]* She told me to stand up straight. Do you think the birds were singing for her?

Vanessa comforts her. Virginia lies down to sleep.

Scene transition. *Vanessa is 17, Virginia is 15.*

VANESSA: *[Rushes as though pushing through busy streets]* Three days a week I escape to my art class. Oh, the delicious happiness of banging the front door behind me and launching into the teeming bustle of the streets! The air fans my cheek as I cycle along Queen's Gate. I tear past strolling couples, nannies with their charges, grey-suited men on their way to work, and feel as if I have a purpose in life.

Vanessa mimes painting or if a painted backdrop is used she paints onto this.

VANESSA: I immerse myself in the conundrum of my picture. I grapple with space and form, light and dark, contour and texture. In the process I forget your pain and Father's misery and Stella's cares.

16

Scene transition. Vanessa seated on the floor next to a box on which the imaginary figure of her brother Thoby is sitting. They are looking at his drawings.

VANESSA: Thoby shows me his drawings. 'These are the ones I started with,' he says. 'I tried out a number of angles,' he says, 'couldn't get the colour right,' he says. I understand exactly. I should like this moment to last forever, but your face appears in the doorway.

VIRGINIA: *[Virginia speaks as though to Thoby]* So there you are! I've been looking for you everywhere. What are you doing? Oh drawings. I'm glad to find you, anyway. I've been rereading "Antony and Cleopatra". Really I don't understand what you mean about Shakespeare's women being such glorious creatures. Come along Thoby and tell me the holes in my argument. It seems to me they are cut out with a pair of scissors. Not so much actual women as a man's tailored view of how women should be.

VANESSA: I know that for the rest of the evening you will monopolise Thoby. Neither of you notice as I pull the door closed.

17

Scene transition. Vanessa reading a letter.

VIRGINIA: A letter! Who is it from?

VANESSA: It's from Margery.

VIRGINIA: Margery! And what is her crisis? I suppose she writes it at great length and with much misspelling. I never met anyone who mangles the English language with such constancy. She merits a prize! Do let's hear it. I could do with some entertainment.

VANESSA: It's private.

VIRGINIA: All the more reason. Private always means something delicious. Come on, let's have it.

VANESSA: Margery has written to me. I don't think I should let you read what she says.

VIRGINIA: You are being unfair. I show you all my letters.

VANESSA: Perhaps it's time we stopped. Perhaps it's time we had interests and friendships outside the family. *[To the audience]* If I let you read the letter you will ridicule and demolish it until there is nothing left to threaten you.

18

Scene transition. *Virginia lies down.*

VANESSA: It is late when I come into our room after the argument. I feel my way towards your bed. As I get closer I see an unexpected shape. To my astonishment I realise it is our brother George. He jumps up at once, he is fighting to control his breath. *[To Virginia]* He didn't - you know... Does George come in here often when I'm downstairs? Does he... try to touch you?

Virginia flies into Vanessa's arms sobbing.

Scene transition. *Vanessa and Virginia are 18 and 16.*

VANESSA: I come into the drawing room swathed in white voile overlaid with black and silver sequins. I have amethysts and opals round my neck and my hair is pinned with enamel butterflies. George raises his eyeglass and appraises me. There is no difference between his gesture and his scrutiny of the Arab mare he has bought for my daily rides. I look to you for protection but you turn away.

The scene shifts slightly to later that evening.

VANESSA:	*[To Virginia]* At the party the rooms are ablaze with light. *[Imitating George and miming a handshake]* 'Mr Chamberlain, allow me to introduce my half-sister, Miss Vanessa Stephen'. Miserably I shake his hand. I can think of nothing to say. George is angry. *[Imitating George]* 'Would you like to tell me what that was about? I suppose you think it's amusing to insult people. Your hair was awful, too!' *[To audience]* Yet as I think back to that time now I cannot blame George entirely. His constant haranguing, his perpetual reminders as to our place and obligations, focused what might otherwise have remained vague longings for an alternative.

Scene transition.

VANESSA:	The noose of domesticity draws round me. Mother and our sister Stella are both gone now and I am their heir. The angel in the house.
VIRGINIA:	Vanessa! Father wants you! Vanessa!

Vanessa hurriedly sorts through some papers and checks her appearance. Virginia sits in imitation of their father, Leslie Stephen.

VANESSA: The accounts, Father.

VIRGINIA: *[Imitating Leslie Stephen]* What's this? Strawberries! You allowed Sophie to order strawberries in May! Salmon! Do you mean to tell me the fish we ate Tuesday last was salmon? Look at the price girl! You stand there like a block of stone! Do you wish to ruin me? Can you not imagine what it's like for me now? Have you no pity?

Virginia turns away.

VANESSA: Sometimes I stab Father, sometimes I smother him with his pillow, sometimes it is the lethal mix of medicines I pour from the vials on his bedside table that kills him. I kill him quickly, effortlessly. I do it without volition and he makes no attempt to resist. It is as if a pact is being played out between us. I walk to the window, pull open the curtains, and let the light flood in. Then I wake up.

Scene transition. *Vanessa and Virginia stand facing each other as though at a graveside. Vanessa and Virginia are 24 and 22.*

21

VANESSA: We stand watching the bearers lower Father into the frozen ground. I realise from the look in your eyes that you are determined to remember him as finer than he was, that you will erase from your memory all his petty tyrannies, his appeals for our sympathy. You sever yourself from reality and retreat again into madness.

Virginia backs away from the grave distraught and points at Vanessa.

VIRGINIA: *[Distressed]* The King stopped outside your window and told you the whole dirty tale. There, there is the culprit. Seize her! The birds sang in Greek, though there was no mistaking their meaning.

Scene transition. *Vanessa is visiting Virginia.*

VANESSA: *[Handing Virginia books]* Here are the books you asked for in your letter, though Dr Savage was quite firm when I spoke to him that you should only read for a very short time each day.

VIRGINIA: *[Listlessly]* Savage would like to wrap me up in cotton wool – or whatever the medical equivalent is. Does he not see that all this is making me ill? Veronal, chloral, paraldehyde. A sleeping draught to overcome the ill-effect of the digitalis. Bromide to ward off the sleeping draught. A tincture for the headache brought on by the bromide. All this to be washed down by 15 glasses of milk a day. You know he wants to pull out my teeth.

Vanessa looks guilty and nods.

VIRGINIA: *[Meekly]* Thank you.

They embrace.

Scene transition. *To be read as letters sent while Virginia is recovering.*

VANESSA: Beloved

VIRGINIA: Dearest Dolphin

VANESSA: We are all thriving here, though your company is sorely missed by all.

VIRGINIA: How much longer must I stay here?

VANESSA: You must be sure to eat and sleep enough so that your strength returns quickly.

23

VIRGINIA:	It's a damnable shame that I'm shut up in the dark again.
VANESSA:	Those voices are certainly figments of your imagination.
VIRGINIA:	I count the days and drink my milk like a good girl.
VANESSA:	You must think me a dreadful old heifer to worry as I do!
VIRGINIA:	I really don't think I can stand much more of this, but of course I'll submit and I'm so sorry to have been such a trouble.
VANESSA:	We are all looking forward to seeing you.
VIRGINIA:	I adore you and miss you. Write to me and say you want me to come home. Please, please bring me home.
VANESSA:	Dolphin.
VIRGINIA:	Yours Billy.

Scene transition.

VANESSA:	*[to Virginia]* Bloomsbury has become so infamous! It's a house we can afford and

24

not in the neighbourhood of our aunts. Space, light, white walls, without clutter. This is our turning point.

[to audience] Time has wrapped layers of myth and envy round what started very simply. A handful of young men, Thoby, Saxon, Lytton, Leonard and Clive and two nervous, ill-at-ease women seated round a fireplace. *[Vanessa and Virginia sit]* I was as entertained as anyone by your originality. We were conspirators once again. I, welcoming and presiding, while you captivated everyone with your eloquence.

VIRGINIA: *[as though speaking to her circle of friends]* As children Nessa and I played in the dark land under the nursery table, in a gloom encircled by firelight, peopled with legs and skirts. We drifted together like ships in an immense ocean and Nessa asked me whether black cats had tails. And I told her they did not.

VANESSA: *[Amused and embarrassed]* Virginia!

VIRGINIA: Then there was her passion for art. When she won the prize at her drawing school, she hardly knew how to tell me in order that I might repeat the news at home.

"They've given me the thing—I don't know why" she said. "What thing?" "O they say I've won it—the book—the prize you know." She was awkward as a long-legged colt.

VANESSA: Virginia please.

VIRGINIA: *[playfully]* Oh, would you rather I talked of myself? Well, I'll tell you all about the French actors instead. *[She continues as though telling a story while Vanessa speaks to the audience]*

VANESSA: *[to audience]* Clive stares at me intently. His eyes hold mine for a moment, and I feel a sudden dizzying exhilaration, like seeing a Tintoretto for the first time. I am voluptuous, a love goddess, carnal and bold. You do not like this unfamiliar sister. *[to Virginia]* But I have rejected Clive's proposal of marriage. I do not want marriage. I do not want to relinquish our new-found freedom. We are only just beginning our journey. I am not ready to turn back yet.

Scene transition. Vanessa is 27, Virginia is 24.

VANESSA: I refuse to accept his death. How can I admit that my brother Julian Thoby Stephen is no more? I stare at his body laid out for burial, dry-eyed. Once again it is your grief that allows me to pass safely over the vortex. I turn my back on the pit of fear and disintegration as you weep. I go on with my life. I write to Clive accepting his proposal.

Scene transition.

VANESSA: It is as if Clive's gentle, practiced fingers slowly stroke away a layer of dull varnish releasing the hues and textures of the paint so the figure comes alive at last. We net life in the warmth of our embraces, and together banish all thoughts of death.

Scene transition. Vanessa helps Virginia out of her coat.

VANESSA: We are enjoying the story you sent us. Clive says he particularly liked the explanatory passages, where the prose was less wrought. He says it had an immediate quality some of the more poetic passages lacked.

VIRGINIA: I often wonder if I shouldn't go with my first thoughts on things. They usually

27

come out more directly. The trouble begins when I read what I've written and realise all the nuances that aren't yet planted in my words.

VANESSA: *[Changing the subject]* Anyway, I need your help with the food. The others will be here soon.

[To the audience] Gwen congratulates me on my picture. Clive puts a record on the gramophone. I feel Clive's arm encircle my waist. *[She dances]* The music finishes and I whisper to Clive to ask you to dance. For a few steps you follow him. Leonard comes to talk to me and when I search for you again you are nowhere to be seen.

[To Virginia] You're not leaving.

VIRGINIA: You set him up to do that. You want to make me look ridiculous.

VANESSA: *[Shrugging]* I thought you would like someone to dance with.

VIRGINIA: I don't want your pity! You're so unfair! You have everything – Clive, money, people wanting your pictures – whereas I have... nothing.

VANESSA: You must see how we all worship you. You'll find someone. You could marry tomorrow if only you would let yourself. Walter is clearly smitten. He can hardly take his eyes off you. And Lytton tells anyone who will listen that you are the most brilliant woman he knows. You're beautiful, Billy. Men are interested in you. All they need is for you to encourage them a little.

Vanessa takes Virginia's arm and leads her away.

Scene transition.

VANESSA: Even I cannot do justice to the awfulness of Clive's family home, Cleeve House. Here, I am a beached dolphin, lashing about for water on the sand. I need your words to revive me. I cannot wait until I see you again. [To Virginia] Here you are. Clive, pour her a glass of wine. How is the novel doing? Clive won't tell me a thing about it.

VIRGINIA: I've been trying to get back to the dream-like quality I had when I started it. I want to show that men and women are different, but I don't want to preach. I quite agree that like God one shouldn't. The effect I

29

want is of running water. Everything fluid
and broad and deep.

VANESSA: *[To audience]* I have a sudden, painful
image of you as a successful writer, sought
after and fêted while my own pictures go
unnoticed. I feel excluded and second-rate.
[To Virginia] Clive and I have been
wondering how your harem is faring! Have
you spoken to Sydney since you refused
him? Clive wonders what kind of creature
you will have.
[To audience] I have played into your
hands. The topic of your suitors has
piqued Clive's interest.

VIRGINIA: Ah! There's the rub. *[Referring to
Vanessa]* First loves are always difficult to
replace. As to whom I should like to make
my life's companion – I do not honestly
know that such a being exists.

VANESSA: *[To audience]* I see now that Clive was a
willing accomplice in your work of
destruction. You accompanied him on his
walks, beguiled him with your stories,
seduced him with your coruscating prose. I
never quite forgave you.

Scene transition. *Vanessa is 28, Virginia is 26.*

30

VANESSA: I keep the slow swell of my belly, the dawning realisation that I am carrying a new life to myself. When I finally break the news to Clive I watch his face alter from pride through fear to regret. [As though cradling a child] The awe of holding my newborn infant. A pact is established between us as I prise open his tiny fingers and feel them curl tight again round mine. It is a promise neither you nor Clive understand. I name him after my beloved brother – Julian Thoby. My Julian.

VIRGINIA: You have forgotten me. Where are my kisses? You have turned your back on me. You have no right to name the baby after our brother. Thoby is not yours to resurrect. You are unkind and selfish and ridiculous!

Scene transition. Vanessa is 30, Virginia is 28

VANESSA: All morning I have sat by the window and watched for the pair of you to come back from your walk. I sooth myself with colour. I only wish to console myself. Suddenly I crave black. I picture your hand resting lightly on Clive's arm; he will try to kiss you. I cannot stop myself from

31

crying. My dear friend Roger Fry understands. I tell Roger about Clive's indifference and how I'm too tired to paint. I tell him my second baby, Quentin, will not gain weight and that I think you are a having an affair with Clive. Roger catches each of my torments and holds them fast.

Scene transition. Virginia wears a headdress to suggest her Cleopatra costume.

VANESSA: You look extraordinary. Disguised as Cleopatra, people crowd round you. I have no costume. I feel awkward and out of place.

Vanessa crosses to Virginia

VIRGINIA: *[Drunk]* So you've come to say hello at last. It's so refreshing to see you without your appendage. I had started to think of your body as permanently misshapen – inseparable from the large, mewling infant you had attached to your hip. As a matter of fact, Ottoline and I were just talking about babies. I was telling her mine will be entirely made of paper. Paper and words. The labour is roughly the same – though there is perhaps more blood in the case of

32

written offspring – but this is amply compensated for by other advantages. After all, books do not grow up and turn their backs on their ageing creators. Now where's that delicious husband of yours? I'm glad you're here. Ott can be so ridiculous! She worships all artists but can never quite decide to set her coronet aside, so everything she says is tinged with an overbearing condescension. Look at her flirting with Clive! She's like some terrifying Medusa, with her great beaky face.

VANESSA: *[To audience]* I do not know whether I am shocked at the way you tear Ottoline to pieces, or relieved that once again you are confiding in me. People have started to hear of you. In some part of myself, I need your triumph. I cradle my baby and take perverse comfort in knowing you are a success. While my ambitions lie dormant, I hope your achievements might stand for us both.

Scene transition.

VANESSA: It is 1910, the First Post Impressionist Exhibition at the Grafton Gallery. I cannot look anymore. I turn to Roger. He understands at once and leads me to a quiet room at the side. He holds me in his arms and I press my face into his jacket. He knows without my saying anything how much this exhibition has meant to me. He says 'you will paint your own masterpieces'.

VIRGINIA: *[Reading the newspaper]* Unskilled, vulgar, offensive! Look at these headlines. *[Quoting]:* 'It is paint run mad... the emotion expressed is too often that of a violent bilious headache... In the large gallery the eye meets Gauguin's primitive, almost barbaric, studies of Tahitian women – bizarre, morbid and horrible'. Well!

VANESSA: The furore Roger's exhibition of French painting is causing in London! I have scarcely ever seen anything so exciting. I feel a flutter of elation in my breast, as if the pictures have touched a chord that has not been sounded until now. How about if we go to the ball dressed as South Sea Islanders? We could be Gauguin's women. What do you think? *[She puts a flower behind her ear]*

VIRGINIA: You look... glorious!

VANESSA: In Constantinople I feel the imprint of my fingers on Roger's skin. I feel the passion of Roger's kiss and the excruciating guilt as my stomach cramps in pain. I see the shape of an infant in the sluice of blood that streams between my legs. The images fizz and blur until all the elements twist together and Roger and Clive and I form part of some hideous beast. It is Roger who brings me back from the precipice. It is his hand that soothes away my terrors, his voice that coaxes me back to life.

Scene transition. *Vanessa is 34, Virginia is 32.*

VANESSA: So, is it true? Clive says Gerald is to publish your novel.

VIRGINIA: Yes.

VANESSA: And will I like it?

VIRGINIA: I hope so... you know most of what I do is for you. I'm afraid I'm a long way behind the painters, though, in understanding design.

VANESSA: We've both had so much to unlearn.

35

VIRGINIA: I think you've gone further than I have. There is no doubt painting is leading the way. Fiction has forgotten its purpose. The novelists circle round their subject, describing everything that is extraneous to it, and then are surprised when it slips from view. Look, there's Roger. Shall we go over?

VANESSA: No, not yet *[Evasively]*. I hear that Leonard Woolf is on his way home from Ceylon. I'd like to find out more about Leonard. By all accounts he has made a great success of his time out there. I gather he is looking for an English wife. He could be just the thing.

[To audience] I sense that I am sending you a life raft. I was the carnal sister, you were the intellectual, so the story runs. The truth is rather different. You experience intimacies in your marriage I can only dream of. Perhaps, if I were able to accept devotion...

Scene transition.

VANESSA: I have the sudden sense that from now on whatever you do will be shared with Leonard before it is confided to me. Leonard's letters are detailed, frank and unflinching. *[Reading]* 'She appears to find lovemaking unappealing'. I reply immediately. *[Writing]* 'She has always been physically unresponsive'. Perhaps if I was more generous, I might help him find the confidence to explore. As it is, my words confirm his fears, and steer you towards a sexless marriage. Fate will punish me for this.

Scene transition. Vanessa is 36, Virginia is 34.

Vanessa holds a copy of The Voyage Out.

VANESSA: I have been expecting it for days. Your first novel. What astonishes me is your audacity. *[reading]* 'We are suffering the tortures of the damned,' said Helen. 'This is my idea of hell,' said Rachel. Here I am again, awkward and ill at ease in my black and white sequined dress. Am I never to escape? This is not literature, it is mere journalism. I no longer mind your pilfering. Now that I am sure you have not written a masterpiece, I can read your words with equanimity.

Scene transition. Virginia poses as Duncan Grant painting.

37

VANESSA: Duncan Grant. Sometimes love comes instantly, with blinding certainty, sometimes it is a sea mist, slowly enveloping the view until one is hard-pressed to remember the features of the shore. I set my own easel alongside Duncan's on the grass. I study him as I mix my colours. *[Vanessa mirrors Virginia's movements]* As I begin to paint, our movements fall into the same pattern. There is no rivalry, only the shared sense of a common pursuit. Not since those far-off days with Thoby in the nursery have I felt so at one with another human being. I cannot help falling in love.

Scene transition.

VANESSA: I find you in the boys' room, sitting in the chair by the window with Quentin on your lap.

VIRGINIA: The fairies had all gathered at the bottom of the garden for their annual flower festival... *[Virginia's voice quietly underscores Vanessa]*

VANESSA: I watch Duncan smoking in the garden. I think how beautiful he looks as he stares up at the sky. When I turn away you are

38

watching me. It is impossible to conceal my love from you.

Scene transition.

VIRGINIA: You're shutting yourself off from reality! You can't just hide your head in the sand and pretend that the war isn't happening!

VANESSA: I had hoped you would support my plan of moving out of London and settling permanently in the country. Do you really think all this writing can make a difference? After all they burned Clive's pamphlet. If anything, it seemed to whip up support for the war. Did I tell you Duncan was showered with white feathers when we walked home from the village last week? It was horrible. Two of the butcher's boys followed us all the way down the street.

VIRGINIA: Just because we're not caught up in all the jingoism doesn't mean we should ignore it. Maynard says that since Kitchener's poster last year, all his brightest students at Cambridge have enlisted. At the very least, we need to work out what all these words that decide our fortunes mean. Besides, in the end, your art will suffer.

39

VANESSA: *[Bristling]* Politics doesn't come into it! When I'm working on a picture what I'm looking for isn't in the world, it's in the relationship between the object in front of me and my marks on the canvas. I never know what it will be when I start working, but I always know when I find it. It's the thing that makes sense of all the rest. It might be an echo – a repetition or movement – or it might be a single joining line. *[Pauses to gauge Virginia's response]* You've put on weight!

VIRGINIA: *[Smiling]* Yes. Leonard did not rule an entire Ceylonese province for nothing. If I eat up all my dishes I am given sweets.

VANESSA: Are you pregnant? I thought you had decided... Leonard wrote to me...

VIRGINIA: What? That he thinks I shouldn't have children. Well and why shouldn't I? Dr Savage doesn't see any harm in it, and says that as long as I'm careful it could do me the world of good. Wouldn't you like to be an aunt?

VANESSA: What about your illness? Isn't there a danger childbirth could bring it on?

VIRGINIA: So you are against me too.

VANESSA: It isn't that. I don't want you to be ill again, that's all. Pregnancy can be very draining. *[Pause]* I should be going. I said I would meet Duncan at the workshop.

Scene transition.

VANESSA: Duncan and I are in London for one of Maynard's suppers. We seat ourselves on either side of a tall, powerfully built young man. Duncan strikes up a conversation with him, intended to put him at his ease. I overhear the young man say that though his name is David his friends call him Bunny. That night he and Duncan become lovers.

Scene transition. Vanessa stands back as though evaluating a painting.

VANESSA: It's Duncan's idea that Bunny should sit for us. Duncan's painting is the study of an attractive, sexually-potent young man, mine is the caricature of a flaccid, pasty-faced boy. Magnetism and vibrancy in Duncan's, a sickly sheen in mine. I realise I have painted my jealousy.

41

Scene transition.

VANESSA: *[Yawns]* I'm sorry. We were all up far too late last night. We let the boys dress up with us and they are still very excited.

VIRGINIA: So I see. Was it a family party?

VANESSA: *[distracted]* No, at least... Bunny's birthday. It was Duncan's idea. Bunny...

VIRGINIA: Ness? What is it?

VANESSA: After the boys had gone to bed Duncan fell asleep on the sofa. As I turned to go to my room, Bunny caught hold of my arm and thanked me for the party. I wished him many happy returns and he kissed me on my cheek. But the kiss did not stop where it should have done and I had to... extricate myself.

VIRGINIA: And you didn't want him?

VANESSA: No, of course not! I know how it must seem to you... as if I am nothing... but sleeping with Bunny would have felt like a violation. *[Cries]*

VIRGINIA: Darling, don't cry. You don't really believe what you are saying. Just look around.

VANESSA: What? The children are out of control, the house is falling down round my ears, my paintings don't sell.

VIRGINIA: Don't you know how much I love coming here? Don't you know I'd give up writing tomorrow if I could exchange it for one tiny piece of all this.

VANESSA: *[to the audience]* Gradually, the scraps of my life – the debris from the party, the children's discarded clothes, my half-finished fireplace – coalesce into a whole. You have made a painting.

Scene transition.

VIRGINIA: *[Reading the paper]* Compulsory conscription for all men between 18 and 41.

VANESSA: One can apply for an exemption. Usually on health grounds. There is some provision for conscientious objectors.

VIRGINIA: *[Scanning the paper]* It's limited, though, and dependent in the first instance on local tribunal.

VANESSA: Bigots whose only motive is self-interest. *[to the audience]* There were two hearings. Duncan and Bunny's appeals were upheld on condition that they engaged in work of 'national importance'. They have been promised work on a farm. All I have to do is find us a house.

Scene transition. Vanessa is 37, Virginia is 35. They are wandering around Charleston Farmhouse.

VANESSA: It seems to have everything I need.

VIRGINIA: And if you take it we will be within easy visiting distance of each other again.

VANESSA: This could be a bedroom for Clive, this a study for Maynard; there are rooms for Duncan and the children, a studio for myself.

VIRGINIA: This door leads to the garden. Marigolds, poppies, foxgloves and cornflowers are already growing in wild profusion.

VANESSA: I can imagine Duncan painting on the
               terrace, guests strolling about the lawn,
               myself vital, enabling, beloved. I'll take
               the house on a long lease. *[sighs with
               satisfaction]* Charleston.

*Scene transition. Vanessa crouches as through painting the
tiles around the fireplace.*

VANESSA: I am in the sitting room, painting the tiles
               round the fireplace when you arrive. I
               have spent the morning gardening and my
               clothes are stained with mud. I listen to
               the children storming the remains of the
               shrubbery with homemade guns as the
               sound of gunfire booms across the channel.

VIRGINIA: Is this meant to be the sea?

VANESSA: I suppose I was thinking about the sea,
               though of course it was the colour and
               pattern I had most clearly in mind.

VIRGINIA: So if you weren't thinking about a
               particular seascape, what did you intend
               this mark to be here? I had assumed it was
               a lighthouse.

45

VANESSA: I'm not sure I meant anything in particular by it, though of course I've no objection to you seeing it as a lighthouse.

VIRGINIA: But if it isn't a lighthouse — or indeed anything specific — why is it there?

VANESSA: The blue needed it, the pattern needed it. It gives the eye something to rest on.

VIRGINIA: So you want to include your audience?

VANESSA: Of course. Though I'm not sure I'm predominantly thinking about a viewer as I paint.

VIRGINIA: I'm glad to hear it. Though actually I worry I don't think enough about my reader. When I write it is because it gives me an opportunity to go further into something — a chance to enter what I would otherwise be excluded from. Whereas you — if I understand you correctly — must confront the opposite problem. You are already inside, and your challenge is to find a point of perspective for those who are outside your work.

VANESSA: Oh Virginia! You make too much of what I'm doing.

46

Virginia turns away as though distracted by Vanessa's sons.

VANESSA: The boys file in and settle themselves on the floor beside you. They spar and jostle for your attention. You tease them about their wild appearance, find sweets for them in your bag. They laugh and clap and hang on your every word. I begin to fear they are growing away from me. When the time comes for you to leave, I watch you walk down the drive, your arm tucked in Leonard's, the boys dancing in attendance behind you.

Scene transition.

VANESSA: I ask you to sit for me. When the features of your face are done I stop and examine the effect. I have failed. I pick up my knife and scrape the paint clear. I gaze at your closed eyelids, the back of your head resting against the chair. I wash the entire oval of your face in a flesh tone. This time your expression is blank. I have painted what you are to me.

Scene transition.

VANESSA: The war edges closer. Its madness infiltrates the house. It steals through

47

doors, seeps between crevices, invisible, contagious, evil. Duncan looks exhausted. I long to take him in my arms. I lie in bed and listen to the wind in the trees, trying not to hear the pounding of the guns across the channel, or the slow tread of Bunny's pacings outside my door. Still he has not given up his desire to sleep with me. There is a sudden shout. I push open the door. There on the floor, many-limbed and monstrous in the candlelight, are the naked writhing bodies of Duncan and Bunny. I see Bunny's fist flail blows on Duncan's chest. Bunny stumbles to his feet, sweating and defensive, blood oozing from a cut on his lip. I help Duncan to his feet, lead him back to my room and cradle him in my arms. He weeps as he buries himself in my flesh. When his seed pumps into me I wonder if it is me or Bunny he is thinking of.

Scene transition. Vanessa is 38, Virginia is 36. Virginia is sitting as though typesetting for the Hogarth Press.

VIRGINIA: Who would have thought Leonard and I would be running our own printing press? I typeset most afternoons. It's actually rather restful, once you get used to it. Of course we had a terrible time getting the machine to work. All we had was an instruction manual and Leonard's rudimentary knowledge of mechanics.

VANESSA: So what sort of books will you print?

VIRGINIA: That all depends on how quickly we can master the art! We're starting with two stories, one by Leonard and one by me. Carrington has done some woodcuts for us. I didn't realise how talented she is until Lytton showed us some of her work. We've already had a go at printing them. Would you like to see? *[Handing Vanessa the pictures]*

VANESSA: How do you plan to use the woodcuts?

VIRGINIA: We can put them on the dust-jacket, as a frontispiece, inside the text. The possibilities are endless.

VANESSA: You mean you can print the woodcuts alongside the words?

VIRGINIA: Yes. It's not that difficult to do. Once I've worked out the space I need for the image I simply set the type around it.

Scene transition.

VANESSA: That night, when everyone is in bed, I get out the story you sent me. As my eyes travel the lines of your prose, my mind races with ideas. I find paper and charcoal. I work quickly, excitedly. Soon I have covered your story with my pictures.

Scene transition.

VANESSA: So, I have another child. Despite all the tribulations of my love for Duncan it has produced this. My daughter sleeps in her crib by my side. I cannot think of a name good enough for her. Clarissa, Rachel, Helen?

VIRGINIA: Angelica.

VANESSA: Angelica. Bunny quips that as soon as she's old enough he will marry her. As he reaches into the crib to lift her, I am seized with a fear that he will steal her too. I think of you, bent over your writing table, drafting your new novel. You have accomplished so much more than me.

Scene transition.

VANESSA: *[to Virginia]* How long have you been unwell?

50

VIRGINIA: I thought I heard a car. How is Angelica? Nessa, I'm so sorry, I've let you down. You know how much I was looking forward to having the boys here. Of course I'd made all sorts of plans for things to do with them. Leonard insisted on calling you.

VANESSA: And you do everything Leonard says?

VIRGINIA: I owe him so much Ness. You can't imagine all he does for me. I just wish that sometimes – he'd let me flex my wings a little.

VANESSA: And what would you do if you could flex your wings?

VIRGINIA: Oh, lots of things. Have children, for instance.

VANESSA: It's not too late.

VIRGINIA: Of course it is! I'm forty.

VANESSA: And I'm forty-two.

VIRGINIA: It's always been easier for you.

VANESSA: I must go and gather up the boys.

51

VIRGINIA: Dearest... You know this isn't how I wanted my life to be.

VANESSA: *[Impatiently changing the subject]* I love the story you're working on with the children.

VIRGINIA: Do you? Perhaps you'll let the boys come and stay once I'm better.

VANESSA: *[To audience]* We sit in the garden of your new country home - Monk's House. The apple trees are in blossom and the breeze scatters pink and white petals at our feet. I watch Julian and Quentin help Leonard remove a dead branch from one of the trees. The branch splinters then plummets to the ground. The boys descend on it with jubilant cheers.

VANESSA: Will it be a good place to write in do you think?

VIRGINIA: I hope so. Actually, I've begun a new novel. Leonard calls it my ghost story.

VANESSA: And who is the ghost?

VIRGINIA: Thoby.

VANESSA: You're writing a novel about Thoby?

VIRGINIA: Yes, I didn't intend to. I began with the
                idea that you can never get inside another
                person's life – not really – and the life that
                came into focus as I wrote was Thoby's.
                [Hesitating] I thought you'd be pleased.

Scene transition.

VANESSA: There is a painting I should like to paint. I
                see it in my mind's eye when I lie awake at
                night. Sometimes it stares back at me as I
                gaze into the fire, or catch glimpses of it
                lodged in the trees as I walk through the
                garden. While it always contains the same
                elements – you, me, the child in the
                highchair, a man, Mother – they
                constantly rearrange themselves.
                Sometimes one of the figures disappears
                altogether. This happens most particularly
                with Mother. Whenever she is absent I
                take her place. I can do nothing to prevent
                this movement. I know that if I block it
                the space will engulf the entire picture.
                Sometimes you are an ally in the picture,
                sometimes a child that requires protection;
                sometimes your proximity is a threat.
                Whenever your opposition becomes too
                powerful I have no choice but to force

53

your retreat. Yet I can't risk losing you altogether. While other parts of the painting emerge and recede without disaster, you are necessary to its equilibrium.

Scene transition. *Virginia takes the role of Duncan Grant*

VANESSA: Duncan has set his easel slightly ahead of mine. As I work, I can see the slope of his head and shoulders, the movement of his hand. I add silver and cerulean to the sky. Duncan says:

VIRGINIA: *[as Duncan Grant]* Bunny will marry, Adrian has married, even Maynard thinks of marrying. They'll all succumb. Except me.

VANESSA: I see the hopeless expression on Duncan's face.

VIRGINIA: *[as Duncan Grant]* Ness, I wish I could...

VANESSA: He wants me to absolve him, to tell him it makes no difference. *[To Virginia as Duncan Grant]* Let's finish our pictures.

Scene transition.

VIRGINIA: I am so envious of the companionable way you and Duncan paint together compared to my solitariness as a writer. You are like brother and sister, fond yet inviolably chaste.

VANESSA: *[To audience]* With the surety of lightening you scissor my sky into halves. Your words leave me shrivelled and exposed. Bunny's defection changes nothing, except that now Duncan pursues his love affairs away from home. My life while Duncan is gone revolves around the post. In the mornings there is a leap of hope as I watch the postman. But there is the day a letter comes full of foreboding: a doctor has diagnosed typhoid. *[Rushing around and gathering anything that comes to hand]* Suddenly I am flying round the house, throwing clothes and wash-things into bags. All I can think as I grasp Angelica by the hand is that I must get to Duncan as quickly as I can. Images of Thoby beat in my head. There are reflections of Thoby's coffin in the grimy carriage windows. When I get there Duncan's mother assures me he is recovering. She leaves the maid to show us the door. I have no status. I am neither wife nor lover, not family or friend.

Scene transition.

VANESSA: I have a recurring dream. In it I am sitting by a window looking out over a garden. Your chair is empty. The only sign that you have been sitting there is the notebook you have laid face down on the grass. I stare at the absence.

Scene transition. The sound of a party. Virginia dancing.

VANESSA: Several couples are already dancing. You catch hold of Vita. As you spin her round you fling your arms above your head, wild and free. Everyone claps as the dance ends. You survey your audience and take a deep bow, your face flushed and ecstatic.

Virginia walks over to Vanessa and flings her arms around her.

VIRGINIA: So, what do you think of her?

VANESSA: She considers me as I imagine an Arab horse might consider a long-eared donkey.

VIRGINIA: *[laughing, she sits and lights a cigarette]* She certainly has pedigree. Did I tell you her ancestors go back to the Norman Conquest? I'm thinking of copying her and

56

getting my hair shingled. Why not? It's time we moved on. Besides, imagine not having to rely on hairpins!

VANESSA: Is that why you're wearing Mother's dress?

VIRGINIA: *[Ignoring the comment]* Be honest, don't you think she's magnificent?

VANESSA: Since you do everything to stir up my jealousy, I shall refuse to answer.

VIRGINIA: *[she swings Vanessa round so that she is seated on her lap]* I do no such thing! We've asked her to do a book for the press. It should do extremely well. She's very much in demand as an author. I wouldn't be surprised if she wins a prize. Actually, I'm thinking of writing a book about her. After all, you always complain if I write about you. I thought I might try something different. Something playful and light. A spoof historical drama, for instance. We could do with new forms for all the old feelings, don't you think? How about Vita as an Elizabethan courtier? I see her moustached and manly – though there again, she'd make a splendidly exotic princess. Anyway, enough of that. *[She*

57

lights a cigarette] Leonard and I are going to rent the villa. So here's to our new life in Cassis!

Vanessa appears displeased.

VIRGINIA: I don't understand your reaction to the villa. After all, you spent most of last summer trying to persuade us to move there!

VANESSA: I'm not sure it would suit you.

VIRGINIA: Nonsense!

VANESSA: What I mean is – your life is very different. You need libraries, people – it doesn't matter where I am as long as...

VIRGINIA: As long as I'm near you. My life in England feels barren – dry – with you gone. You make the world dance. *[They begin to dance 'The Charleston']*

VANESSA: Don't be silly! You'll manage perfectly well without me. After all, with me gone, you can do what you like best. *[Planting a kiss on her cheek]* You can invent me to your heart's content.

58

Scene transition.

VANESSA: Angelica sees it first, pointing excitedly as the moth flies in through the open window. We fall silent as it circles the room. I have never seen such a large specimen before. I try to catch it for Julian's collection: a butterfly net and chloroform. That night, as I lie awake, I seem to hear the soft flutter of wings circling the ceiling above my head. I think about Angelica's plea for mercy. I remember Stella, Thoby, mother. How preposterous their dying seemed. I open the window and feel the cool air flood the room. I take the net over to the window and shake the moth gently free. I remain for some time watching in vain for the moth's flight.

VIRGINIA: Is it dead?

VANESSA: I think so. I tried to let it go, though I didn't see it fly away.

VIRGINIA: What wouldn't you do for those brats of yours! I sometimes think you'd boil me in oil if it afforded them pleasure. Cocoa?

VANESSA: *[Nods]* I remember Father's collection of moths. Everything in strict alphabetical order. I used to think that was what adult life was like. Everything organised and in its place. My adult life has turned out exactly the opposite. Bits and pieces, like the scraps of sewing at the bottom of Mother's workbasket. Nothing finished, nothing made whole.

VIRGINIA: At least you have all the strands. They're in your hands.

VANESSA: By that reckoning every adult life's a success!

VIRGINIA: No, Ness. You hold the light. Then there are lonely moths like me circling the lamp, searching for a way in.

VANESSA: I knew you'd make a scene out of it! So what about all the other people sitting round the table tonight? How do they feature in your sketch?

VIRGINIA: They personify the different voices – emblematised by the moth.

VANESSA: Sounds like the start of one of your novels.

Scene transition.

VIRGINIA: *[calling]* Vanessa?

VANESSA: I cannot stop the pictures forming in my mind. I push my stick into the river and watch the water eddy round it in fast-moving circles. If I close my eyes all I see is Duncan's face, smiling as he leans close to his latest lover. I step into the water and feel the icy cold seep into my shoes. The river is shallow near the bank and brown with mud. I feel calmer now that I am in the water, as if the cold is slowly numbing my pain. This is what I desire. Not to feel any more. Not to long for what I cannot have. I let the current catch hold of me. I surrender willingly as the river pulls me from my feet.

VIRGINIA: *[calling]* Vanessa?

VANESSA: I do not know how long I remain in the water. All I can think of is Duncan's declaration that he can never make love to me again.

VIRGINIA: *[calling]* Nessa? Vanessa?

61

VANESSA: I stare at the racing water and long to be released into its embrace. Yet something – fear, is it? – holds me back. Beaten, I crawl, panting and exhausted back to Charleston.

Virginia rushes to Vanessa who has collapsed.

VIRGINIA: Ness, darling. Whatever's happened to you? You're soaking wet. And covered in blood. Have you had an accident? Did you fall in the river? Oh, my God! What have you done? Why didn't you come to me? I can't bear to think what might have happened. I always picture you happy – in the centre of things.

VANESSA: I want you to promise me that you will never tell anyone about this.

VIRGINIA: I promise – if you agree to promise something in return. I want you to swear that no matter what happens – no matter how terrible life seems – you will never try anything like this again. *[Vanessa nods]* Brandy, that's what you need!

Scene transition.

VANESSA: *[to Virginia]* I am working on two large canvases simultaneously. In this picture, we can see an elegantly dressed woman perching on a footstool in front of a fire. She's gazing at the naked figure of a small boy, her son, we suppose.

VIRGINIA: *[Looking at the painting]* It's strange there is a coolness in her look, an aloofness, as if she's holding something in check.

VANESSA: This second woman on the right is seated on a sofa with a much smaller child; she's more engaged with the child she's holding. Do you see? But something about the way she looks at the boy tells us she will soon depart.

VIRGINIA: There's resignation and wistfulness in her expression. She is studying the child far too intently, Nessa. Must she detach herself if she is to refrain from loving it?

VANESSA: *[Ignoring Virginia and indicating the second picture]* There are no children in this second picture. On the left a nude reclines, while on the right, the woman is fully dressed, staring at the arrangement of fruit on the table before her.

63

VIRGINIA: Whatever she finds in that fruit bowl is preoccupying her entirely!

VANESSA: I cannot finish this picture. There's something vacant at its heart. I'm beginning to sense that neither of the women is central to the painting: whatever work of art they are creating seems somehow beyond their reach. Something in the women's demeanour implies that I am responsible for their failure, that it is my task to alter their fate. Yet I scarcely know how.

Scene transition. Vanessa is 55, Virginia is 53.

VIRGINIA: You've given us all a terrible fright.

VANESSA: How long have I been like this?

VIRGINIA: Two days. You collapsed on the terrace after the news of Roger's death and we decided the best thing would be to keep you here.

VANESSA: I can't bear the thought that I'll never be able to talk to him again. Images of him dance before me. I remember his energy, the bright music of his voice. I spurned his love, took his friendship for granted.

64

VIRGINIA: I've been reading his last letter. He wrote it after staying with you at Charleston. He writes about you... the unique atmosphere you create round you – he says the beauty of your way of life sustains him.

VANESSA: Will you read to me?

VIRGINIA: Of course. *[She begins to read from T S Eliot's 'The Waste Land']*

Scene transition.

VANESSA: *[to audience]* My son Julian's letters from China become the highpoint of my week. It is as if the distance between us, the fact that we can only communicate by writing, encourages us to reveal more about ourselves then we have ever dared to before. Now it is Julian offering me advice, Julian pledging love and support. Life unfurls through my son.

VIRGINIA: We've had letters from Julian. One for Leonard and one for me. They came yesterday.

VANESSA: What does he say? Is he well?

VIRGINIA: He sounds as if he's hell-bent on proving himself. Leonard's letter particularly is all about politics. He wants to use the Labour Party as a platform for an armed revolution – and he wants Leonard to help him do it! He thinks decisive military action is the only hope for Spain.

VANESSA: Is that what you and Leonard think? It seems to contradict everything we struggled for during the last war. *[Pause]* I'm worried about Julian.

VIRGINIA: Why?

VANESSA: Everything he says is so black and white. I'm worried the distance – the fact that he's isolated and so far away – means the reality of the situation is lost on him.

VIRGINIA: Do you remember the war games he and Quentin used to play when they were little? That's what his letters remind me of now. The frustrations of a small boy, dressed up as military strategy. How does a young man surrounded by a family who adore him ever succeed in breaking free?

VANESSA: Sometimes I think everything I do ends up damaging them. It's as if I can't see them as separate people – only as part of myself. The best part. Billy, will you write to Julian for me? Persuade him that no matter what happens he mustn't go to Spain? I don't think I could bear it if anything happened to him.

Scene transition.

VANESSA: This is my picture of Julian's final day. Waking early, the sun already hot, and taking advantage of a lull in the fighting to fill in some of the potholes that obstruct the route to the front. Diving for cover as a group of enemy planes appear, their gunfire whipping the road into dust. A shell exploding near the ambulance where Julian has taken refuge. The shock as a fragment of casing sears into his flesh. The attempt to write to me, three hastily-scribbled words on an empty page of his notebook. When the telephone call comes I cannot take in what the voice is telling me. The blood pounds in my ears, my breath heaves in painful gasps. After that, everything is black, as if the water has closed round me at last. *[She clings to Virginia]* Once again you save me. You, sitting by my bed, stringing your words. I

67

cling to them as to a lifeline. I cannot think, I cannot speak, I can only listen.

VIRGINIA: The world is a work of art and though there is no God we are parts of the design.

Scene transition.

Virginia begins to clear the stage of props as though tidying after an air-raid.

VANESSA: Was the damage from the air-raid very bad?

VIRGINIA: Oh, everything smashed. Furniture, paintings, rugs, all destroyed. The books and papers were almost the only things that survived.

VANESSA: I'm sorry about the house.

VIRGINIA: Don't be. In many ways it's a relief to be free of all those possessions. I've made discoveries too. Look, here's the diary I kept while I was writing *To the Lighthouse*.

VANESSA: Billy, there's something I want to say.

VIRGINIA: *[Looking at a letter]* Ah, these are the letters you wrote to me just before Julian was born. Cleeve House! Do you remember old Squire Bell? That horse's hoof he had made into an ashtray. What a way to commemorate your favourite animal! *[She thrusts the letters into Vanessa's hands]*

VANESSA: Billy. Do you remember that promise I made you?

[To audience] You ignore me. Your body feels frail in my arms as I kiss you goodbye. For a moment I long to stay, to stretch out beside you in front of the fire, feeding you thick slices of toast as I did when we were girls. Instead, I walk to my car and drive away.

Scene transition.

VANESSA: You were the one with the words. If you were here you would know how to tell this tale. You would find a way of penetrating to the truth and enclosing what you found in words of such poetry that one's heart would sing, even as it wept. You walk along the bank searching for stones to fill your pockets. I think of you that day, staring into the fast-flowing river, the still leafless branches of the trees etched

69

against the ghostly grey of the sky. I try to picture what went on inside your head. Did you remember me, Leonard, the children, as you left your stick on the bank and strode out into the swirling water, or were your thoughts bent on escaping what you could no longer bear to endure? I feel the paralysing cold as you wade in, the weight of your wet clothes as you force yourself forward. The water is in my mouth, my lungs, as the river drags us under. This time I cannot escape. The darkness has engulfed the picture.

[Pause] There, it is done. *[The sheets of paper that Virginia has given Vanessa become the story she has written. As she speaks she gently releases the pages one-by-one]* I walk to the river and dip the first sheet of paper in the water. The words blur. The current snatches it from my fingers and rushes it downstream. When the last page has been released I make my dedication. This story is for you.

End